GOOD
OLD-FASHIONED
VALUES

First published in 2025 by OH
An Imprint of HEADLINE PUBLISHING GROUP LIMITED

1

Disclaimer:

Cataloguing in Publication Data is available from the British Library

ISBN 978-1-03542-250-0

Compiled and written by: Jason Ward
Editorial: Saneaah Muhammad
Designed and typeset in Avenir by: Stephen Cary
Project manager: Russell Porter
Production: Marion Storz
Printed and bound in China

MIX
Paper | Supporting
responsible forestry
FSC® C104740

Headline's policy is to use papers that are natural,
renewable and recyclable products and made from
wood grown in well-managed forests and other
controlled sources. The logging and manufacturing
processes are expected to conform to the
environmental regulations of the country of origin.

HEADLINE PUBLISHING GROUP LIMITED
An Hachette UK Company
Carmelite House, 50 Victoria Embankment, London EC4Y 0DZ

The authorised representative in the EEA is Hachette Ireland, 8 Castlecourt Centre,
Dublin 15, D15 XTP3, Ireland (email: info@hbgi.ie)

www.headline.co.uk   www.hachette.co.uk

GOOD OLD-FASHIONED VALUES

THE LITTLE GUIDE TO
FAMILY GUY
UNOFFICIAL AND UNAUTHORIZED

CONTENTS

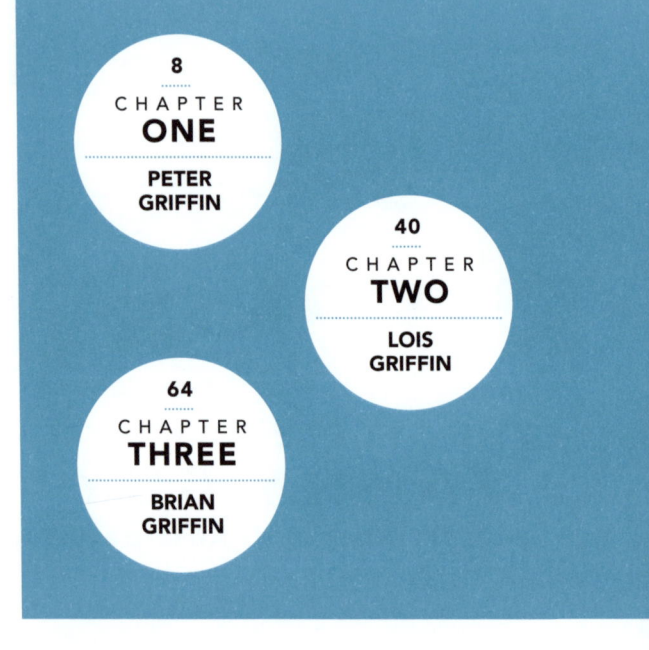

INTRODUCTION

You shouldn't be reading this book, because *Family Guy* shouldn't still be here. It seems inconceivable now, after four hundred episodes and over a quarter of a century, but the show was first cancelled in 2000 and then again in 2002. After premiering on the Fox network in January 1999, it was much-loved but little-seen, programmed against TV juggernauts and shunted around to different nights and time slots. It wasn't until audiences discovered its first three seasons on DVD that *Family Guy* came back from the dead (or temporarily bested a relentless giant chicken).

The main reason it escaped the network's clutches – much like a certain greased-up deaf guy – is the same reason it went from being a cult phenomenon to one of the longest running and most successful animated shows of all time: it is relentlessly funny. Creator Seth MacFarlane's blend of irreverent wit, pop culture references and eagerness to push boundaries continues to find new viewers, some born long after *Family Guy* started airing (then stopped airing, then started again, then stopped again, then started again, clutching its knee and wincing the whole time). While it was famously skewered by its rival *South Park* for its non-sequitur approach to jokes, this has serendipitously made it uniquely suited to being watched, and shared, in chunks online.

Beyond the envelope-pushing jokes, patience-pushing gags and absurdist cutaway wisecracks, however, there's something else behind *Family Guy*'s longevity: its characters have deepened over the years, becoming like old friends. *Good Old-Fashioned Values* is an attempt to capture the show's essence: its wit, ridiculousness and occasionally profound observations. For the true experience, you should probably also take a random break to watch Conway Twitty performing "I See the Want To in Your Eyes" in its entirety.

CHAPTER
ONE

PETER GRIFFIN

It seems today that
all you see…
Is violence in movies
and sex on TV…

66

I may be an idiot, but there's one thing I'm not, sir, and that is an idiot.

99

Peter barters with a used-car salesman.

Season 5, Episode 3: "Hell Comes to Quahog"
"*Family Guy*: 20 Best Peter Griffin Quotes Ranked", screenrant.com

I can be just as non-competitive as anybody. Matter of fact, I'm the most non-competitive. So I win.

Peter runs against Lois to be the head of the School Board of Education.

Season 2, Episode 10: "Running Mates"
"Family Guy: Peter Griffin's 20 Best Quotes", movieweb.com

FACTILY GUY

The origins of *Family Guy* can be found in Seth MacFarlane's thesis film at the Rhode Island School of Design: *The Life of Larry*, a 10-minute short about Larry Cummings, his wife Lois, son Milt and his talking dog Steve.

> **"**
>
> Lois might be worth a million dollars to you, but to me she's worthless. **"**

Peter refuses a bribe from Lois' father.

Season 3, Episode 6: "Death Lives"
"*Family Guy*: 20 Best Peter Griffin Quotes Ranked", screenrant.com

You know what really grinds my gears? People in the nineteenth century. Why don't they get with the freaking programme? It's called an automobile, folks. It's much faster than a horse!

Peter gets a presenting job at Quahog 5.

Season 4, Episode 28: "Stewie B. Goode"
"Family Guy: Peter's 5 Funniest Quotes (& Lois' 5 Funniest)", screenrant.com

"

Lois: Have you been drinking?
Peter: Why yes I have,
thank you.

"

Peter misinterprets Lois' question.

Season 2, Episode 20: "Wasted Talent"
"How To Drink Like Peter Griffin From *Family Guy*", thrillist.com

Then what am I supposed to do with my great ideas? Put them in a tub and clean myself with them? Because that's what soap is for, Lois.

Peter responds to Lois pointing out that he is acting more like a theatre director than a producer.

Season 2, Episode 7: "The King Is Dead"
tvfanatic.com

Brian: Peter, that drink will kill you!
Peter: Brian, whatever kills me makes me stronger.

Peter tries to make his own energy drink.

Season 9, Episode 8: "New Kidney in Town"
"60 Best *Family Guy* Quotes We Love", toynk.com

Jeez, Lois. I spent all morning on a boat drinking beer, telling jokes and screwing around. How about a little me time?

Peter needs to relax after all his relaxing.

Season 1, Episode 4: "Mind Over Murder"
"How To Drink Like Peter Griffin From *Family Guy*", thrillist.com

FACTILY GUY

Impressed by Seth MacFarlane's work on *The Life of Larry*, his Rhode Island School of Design professor submitted the film to Hanna-Barbera, an animation studio and production company, where MacFarlane subsequently worked on shows including *Dexter's Laboratory* and *Johnny Bravo*.

Well, you guys, we did it. We finally went to a restaurant without somebody yelling at us and the rest of the place applauding them.

Peter congratulates his family.

Season 11, Episode 20: "Farmer Guy"
"20 *Family Guy* Quotes and Jokes for the Show's 20th Anniversary",
parade.com

I have an idea so smart that my head would explode if I even began to know what I was talking about.

Peter comes up with another wild plan.

Season 2, Episode 5: "Love Thy Trophy"
"*Family Guy*: 20 Best Peter Griffin Quotes Ranked", screenrant.com

I got drunk and then got my picture taken, so that way when I get pulled over for drunk driving, I look the same as on my licence.

Peter outwits the traffic police.

Season 7, Episode 10: "Fox-y Lady"
"Peter Griffin Quotes That Will Make You Laugh Every Time", ranker.com

How can I be a DJ? I'm just a guy with a laptop and an inflated self-image.

Peter is invited to become a disc jockey.

Season 15, Episode 12: "Peter's Def Jam"
"Family Guy: 20 Best Peter Griffin Quotes Ranked", screenrant.com

Peter: Whoa! Is that really the blood of Christ?
Priest: Yes.
Peter: Man, that guy must have been wasted twenty-four hours a day, huh?

Peter has some communion wine at church.

Season 1, Episode 1: "Death Has a Shadow"
"How To Drink Like Peter Griffin From *Family Guy*", thrillist.com

I guess we've learned that
no matter who you are
or where you're from, life is
a terrible thing.

Peter sums up his new epiphany.

Season 9, Episode 13: "Trading Places"
"*Family Guy*: Peter Griffin's 20 Best Quotes, Ranked", movieweb.com

Peter: Why did all the dinosaurs die out?
Museum tour guide: Because you touch yourself at night.

Peter has a flashback to the last time he felt crappy.

Season 2, Episode 20: "Wasted Talent"
"Top 10 Best *Family Guy* Quotes", thetoptens.com

Pea... Tear... Griffin.
Yeah yeah, Peter Griffin.

Peter struggles to create a fake name for himself based on the objects in his sight.

Season 3, Episode 1: "The Thin White Line"
"Peter Griffin's 10 Weirdest Quotes In *Family Guy*", cbr.com

Tough guy: Smells like this guy's already wet himself.
Peter: Don't flatter yourself, that was from this morning.

Peter stands up to a tough guy.

Season 12, Episode 16: "Herpe the Love Sore"
"Peter Griffin Quotes", quotecatalog.com

It's like I died and went to heaven. But then they realized it wasn't my time yet, so they sent me to a brewery.

Peter wins a ticket to tour the Pawtucket Beer Factory.

Season 2, Episode 20: "Wasted Talent"
"How To Drink Like Peter Griffin From *Family Guy*", thrillist.com

Lois: Peter, you've never done a creative thing in your life.

Peter: That's not true. I wrote *Bonfire of the Vanities.*

Lois: No you didn't.

Peter: …You win this round, Lois.

Peter tries to win an argument with Lois.

Season 2, Episode 7: "The King Is Dead"
imdb.com

66

Any problem caused by a tank can be solved by a tank.

99

Peter makes a fine point.

Season 5, Episode 3: "Hell Comes to Quahog"
"Peter Griffin Quotes", quotecatalog.com

FACTILY GUY

Seth MacFarlane has said that Peter's voice is based on a security guard who worked at the Rhode Island School of Design

It's unknown whether the security guard ever fought with his talking dog over a toy rope.

Mr. Weed? I can't come to work today. I was in a terrible plane crash. My entire family was killed, and I am a vegetable. I'll see you tomorrow.

Peter calls his boss to skip work for the day.

Season 3, Episode 3: "Mr. Griffin Goes to Washington"
familyguy.fandom.com

A boat's a boat but the mystery box could be anything. It could even be a boat!

Peter is given the choice between winning a boat and a mystery box.

Season 2, Episode 8: "I Am Peter, Hear Me Roar"
"Peter Griffin's 10 Weirdest Quotes In *Family Guy*", cbr.com

Let's go drink until we can't feel feelings any more.

Peter is ready for a night out.

Season 3, Episode 19: "Stuck Together, Torn Apart"
Family Guy: 20 Best Peter Griffin Quotes Ranked", screenrant.com

There's a message in my Alpha-Bits. It says 'Oooooo.'

Peter misidentifies his Cheerios as Alpha-Bits.

Season 1, Episode 6: "The Son Also Draws"
"Family Guy: 20 Best Peter Griffin Quotes Ranked", screenrant.com

Well, last night me and Brian got drunk and ate the turkey, but before you get mad we also ate the salad.

Peter tells Lois what happened to the Thanksgiving turkey.

Season 13, Episode 5: "Turkey Guys"
"How To Drink Like Peter Griffin From *Family Guy*", thrillist.com

Lois, this family believes in the Easter Bunny. He died for our sins in that helicopter crash.

Peter struggles to understand his faith.

Season 8, Episode 2: "Family Goy"
"Peter Griffin Quotes", quotecatalog.com

"

Lois: So, Chris, what's the latest with
  your little girlfriend?
Chris: Oh, I don't think Mrs. Lockhart
  likes me at all.
Lois: Mrs. Lockhart? Your teacher?
Peter: Whoa, whoa, whoa, whoa,
  whoa, whoa, whoa, whoa, whoa,
  whoa, whoa, whoa. Lois, this
  is not my Batman glass.

"

Peter is definitely listening to the conversation.

Season 4, Episode 2: "Fast Times at Buddy Cianci Jr. High"
Family Guy: 20 Best Peter Griffin Quotes Ranked", screenrant.com

CHAPTER
TWO

LOIS GRIFFIN

But where are
those good old-
fashioned values…

On which we used
to rely?

The secret to happiness is burying all your true feelings and living a life of bland compromise.

Lois explains her core philosophy.

Season 14, Episode 7: "Hot Pocket-Dial"
"*Family Guy*: Peter's 5 Funniest Quotes (& Lois' 5 Funniest)", screenrant.com

Well, the best advice I can give is: you never know who's gonna grow up to be famous, so just make yourself available.

Lois gives advice on public-access television.

Season 3, Episode 20: "Road to Europe"
"60 Best *Family Guy* Quotes We Love", toynk.com

FACTILY GUY

Seth MacFarlane attended
a New England prep school
called the Kent School.
After *Family Guy* premiered,
its headmaster started a
letter-writing campaign in
an attempt to get the show
cancelled, believing that it
was making fun of the family
of his secretary, Elaine Griffin.

"

Peter, jamming yourself
into a grapefruit is not
an affair.

"

Lois responds to Peter's confession of cheating.

Season 12, Episode 17: "The Most Interesting Man in the World"
"60 Best *Family Guy* Quotes We Love", toynk.com

I had such a crush on her.
Until I met you, Lois. You're my
silver medal.

Lois listens to Peter's story about asking his high school
crush to prom.

Season 2, Episode 14: "Let's Go to the Hop"
"Peter Griffin's 10 Weirdest Quotes In *Family Guy*", cbr.com

Lois: Peter, you're drunk again.
Peter: No, I'm just exhausted
    because I stayed up all
    night drinking.

Lois hears out Peter's logic.

Season 2, Episode 20: "Wasted Talent"
"How To Drink Like Peter Griffin From *Family Guy*", thrillist.com

Lois: Meg, you're a sweet, beautiful girl. He'll come around.

Meg: That's such a Mom answer.

Lois: Well, have you tried showing him the goods? How's that for a Mom answer?

Lois and Meg have a heart-to-heart.

Season 1, Episode 6: "A Hero Sits Next Door"
"*Family Guy*: Meg Griffin's Best Quotes, Ranked", movieweb.com

Lois: Peter, you can't drive the car over that. You're gonna get hurt.

Peter: Lois, I don't come down to Burger King and tell you how to do your job.

Lois: Peter, I don't work at Burger—

Peter: I don't work at burgagaga… I'm busy. Now if you'll excuse me, I have some death to defy.

Lois expresses frustration at Peter's plan to become a daredevil.

Season 5, Episode 9: "Road to Rupert"
familyguy.fandom.com

Lois: Peter, why are we stopped?

Peter: Yeah, I'll have three cheeseburgers.

Lois: Peter, for God's sakes, she's having a baby!

Peter: Oh that's right… and a kid's meal.

Lois and Peter visit a drive-through while taking a pregnant woman to hospital.

Season 3, Episode 11: "Emission Impossible"
"Peter Griffin Quotes", allgreatquotes.com

Lois: I care about the size of your penis as much as you care about the size of my breasts.
Peter: Oh my God! [*Peter runs off crying*].

Lois tries to console Peter.

Season 3, Episode 5: "And the Wiener Is..."
"Louis Griffin Quotes", allgreatquotes.com

This is a man who thinks the plural of goose is sheep.

Lois debates against Peter in an election.

Season 2, Episode 10: "Running Mates"
"60 Best *Family Guy* Quotes We Love", toynk.com

Meg: Mom, I can't clean – I got stuff to do!
Lois: Sweetheart, we all know you don't have any stuff to do.

Lois shoots straight.

Season 2, Episode 21: "Fore, Father"
"20 *Family Guy* Quotes and Jokes for the Show's 20th Anniversary",
parade.com

Peter, breakfast for dinner is anarchy!

Lois, on a phone call with Peter after he visits a dining hall that serves breakfast for dinner.

Season 11, Episode 11: "The Giggity Wife"
"*Family Guy*: Peter's 5 Funniest Quotes (& Lois' 5 Funniest)", screenrant.com

FACTILY GUY

In *Family Guy*'s original pilot, Lois had blonde hair rather than red.

Seth MacFarlane was only given a budget of $50,000 to make the pilot – so perhaps the red ink cost too much money?

Peter, we have a hamper.
Stop throwing your dirty clothes
in the toilet.

Lois is frustrated by Peter's approach to housework.

Season 2, Episode 18: "The Work Song Nanocluster"
tvfanatic.com

Don't forget: if you screw this up, Mommy's going to kill all of your toys.

Lois shows Stewie some tough love.

Season 14, Episode 11: "The Peanut Butter Kid"
"60 Best *Family Guy* Quotes We Love", toynk.com

Here's a little tip: If your instinct tells you to do something, don't do it. If your instinct tells you not to do something, it's probably the right thing to do!

Lois exasperatedly gives Peter some advice.

Season 7, Episode 4: "Baby Not on Board"
tvfanatic.com

66

Lois: Uh, Meg, I got 16 candles for your birthday cake. How does that sound?

Meg: That's not right.

Lois: So… less… more… too many… not enough?

Meg: You stupid son of a bitch! You don't even know how old I am!

Lois: Meg, that kind of language is not appropriate for a girl your age… or is it?

99

Lois definitely knows how old Meg is.

Season 5, Episode 9: "Peter's Two Dads"
imdb.com

FACTILY GUY

In 2009, *Family Guy* became the first animated series since *The Flintstones* in 1961 to be nominated for Outstanding Comedy Series at the Emmys.

"

Man: Wow, Lois Griffin. Hey, I love your act! Nice melons.
Peter: Hey, listen, pal!
Lois: Peter, I'm holding melons.
Peter: Oh.
Man: And her hooters ain't bad either.
Peter: Now hang on a second there.
Lois: Peter! I'm holding hooters!
Peter: Oh, sorry.
Man: No problem… Your wife's hot.
Peter: All right that's it!

"

Lois starts singing publicly and is spotted by an appreciative fan at the supermarket.

Season 1, Episode 4: "Mind Over Murder"
"Louis Griffin Quotes", allgreatquotes.com

Lois: Peter, where have you been?
    You left for the market six hours ago.
    Did you get the beans?
Peter: Lois, I've got something better.
    You know how you've always wanted
    a real diamond engagement ring?
Lois: Oh my God!
Peter: That's right, I bought
    a horse!

Lois' hopes are crushed as Peter proves that romance is actually dead.

Season 7, Episode 8: "Family Gay"
"Peter Griffin Quotes That Will Make You Laugh Every Time", ranker.com

Wow, we rolled three gutter balls on these kids, huh?

Lois faces the hard truth.

Season 14, Episode 13: "An App a Day"
"*Family Guy*: Peter's 5 Funniest Quotes (& Lois' 5 Funniest)", screerant.com

CHAPTER
THREE

BRIAN GRIFFIN

Lucky there's a
Family Guy…

Lucky there's a
man who…

Hey, barkeep, whose leg do you have to hump to get a dry Martini around here?

Brian is ready for another drink.

Season 1, Episode 2: "I Never Met the Dead Man"
"15 Brian Griffin Quotes That Will Help You Get Through Today", metro.co.uk

You know, it's times like this where I think if I didn't talk and you were a normal baby, we wouldn't have any of these problems.

Brian makes a reasonable point.

Season 14, Episode 2: "Papa Has a Rollin' Son"
"The Best Brian Griffin Quotes", ranker.com

FACTILY GUY

Oscar-nominated actor William H. Macy auditioned for the role of Brian, but lost the role to *Family Guy*'s creator, Seth MacFarlane.

> **Peter:** I'll handle it, Lois. I read a book about this sort of thing once.
> **Brian:** Are you sure it was a book? Are you sure it wasn't *nothing*?

Brian calls out Peter on the origins of his plan.

Season 2, Episode 9: "If I'm Dyin', I'm Lyin'"
"15 Brian Griffin Quotes That Will Help You Get Through Today",
metro.co.uk

"

Lois: Together we can do anything.
   Face any foe, overcome any obstacle.
Peter: Yeah, climb any mountain, rent
   any video, dial any phone, and not just
   our phone, Lois, other people's phones,
   decent phones, God-fearing phones,
   phones that everybody else gave up on,
   but we know better, cause we're a team!
Brian: What the hell are you talking
   about?

"

Brian is confused by Peter's motivational speech.

Season 2, Episode 16: "There's Something About Paulie"
"Louis Griffin Quotes", allgreatquotes.com

> I'm not drunk! I just have speech impediment... and a stomach virus... and an inner ear infection.

Brian denies being inebriated.

Season 2, Episode 13: "Road to Rhode Island"
"15 Brian Griffin Quotes That Will Help You Get Through Today",
metro.co.uk

Peter: How much for the gloves?
Brian: Peter, those are yours.
Peter: Ten bucks! Two! Seven! Four! Five-fifty! Ten! Sold! Sucker. I would have gone to fifteen, easy. I am so stupid.

Brian lets Peter haggle for his own gloves.

Season 5, Episode 9: "Road to Rupert"
familyguy.fandom.com

Brian: I was having fun, making new friends, getting laid all the time, sleeping like a rock – but you made the call. You unilaterally decided I was better off a bitter alcoholic failure who could only hang out with a baby.

Stewie: Hey! We have fun.

Brian is disappointed after an operation that turns him back into his old self.

Season 13, Episode 8: "Our Idiot Brian"
"The Best Brian Griffin Quotes", ranker.com

If there were a God… would he give you a smoking hot mom like Lois and then have you grow up looking like Peter?

Brian tries to convert Meg to atheism.

Season 7, Episode 11: "Not All Dogs Go to Heaven"
familyguy.fandom.com

Hey, how about a little less questions and a little more shut the hell up?

Brian is on a serious bender.

Season 3, Episode 1: "The Thin White Line"
"15 Brian Griffin Quotes That Will Help You Get Through Today",
metro.co.uk

Stewie: Now, why in the world would you be embarrassed about dating her?

Jillian: Oh my God, Brian. I was watching something on TV about this guy named Hitler. Somebody should stop him!

Brian is embarrassed by his new girlfriend.

Season 5, Episode 5: "Whistle While Your Wife Works"
imdb.com

FACTILY GUY

Family Guy is famous for its running gags, but one of its lesser-known ones is that the phrase "What the hell?" appears in every episode.

Lois: I'm so bored without Stewie around, I don't know what to do.
Brian: We could get hammered.

Brian suggests a way to pass the time.

Season 2, Episode 15: "Dammit Janet"
imdb.com

❝

You're like all the worst parts of a girlfriend.

❞

Brian and Stewie have a… complicated relationship.

Season 14, Episode 6: "Peter's Sister"
"*Family Guy*: Stewie's 5 Funniest Quotes (& Brian's 5 Funniest)",
screenrant.com

Brian: Seriously, who buys a novelty fire extinguisher?

Peter: I'll tell you who: someone who cares enough about physical comedy to put his entire family into serious danger, that's who.

Brian questions Peter's unhelpful safety purchases.

Season 3, Episode 16: "A Very Special Family Guy Freakin' Christmas"
"20 *Family Guy* Quotes and Jokes for the Show's 20th Anniversary", parade.com

Peter: You want a beer?
Brian: Peter, it's 11 a.m.
Peter: If the clock ain't digital,
you don't know that!

Brian and Peter start early.

Season 13, Episode 8: "Our Idiot Brian"
"How To Drink Like Peter Griffin From *Family Guy*", thrillist.com

How you coming on that novel you're working on? Huh? Got a big stack of papers there? Got a nice little story you're working on there? Your big novel you've been working on for three years? Huh? Got a compelling protagonist? Yeah? Got an obstacle for him to overcome? Huh? Little story brewing there? Working on that for quite some time? Huh?

Stewie mocks Brian about his novel's slow progress.

Season 4, Episode 7: "Brian the Bachelor"
"14 of Stewie's Best Insults on *Family Guy*", cracked.com

66

Brian: You've been hanging out with Tom Cruise?

Stewie: Sure have. We spent the whole day together, and he showed me there are a lot of advantages to being short.

Brian: Oh yeah? Like what? You're the last one to get wet when it rains?

99

Brian teases Stewie about his height.

Season 14, Episode 2: "Papa Has a Rollin' Son"
"The Best Brian Griffin Quotes", ranker.com

Brian: You are getting a little old for a teddy bear.
Stewie: Brian, I'm one.
Brian: Still?

Brian can't comprehend that Stewie is still only one years old.

Season 5, Episode 9: "Road to Rupert"
"Brian Griffin Quotes", quotecatalog.com

66

Hey, what's the point in waiting? You gotta live life while you can, and live it hard.

99

Brian gives Stewie some good advice.

Season 4, Episode 19: "Brian Sings and Swings"
"15 Brian Griffin Quotes That Will Help You Get Through Today", metro.co.uk

CHAPTER
FOUR

CHRIS GRIFFIN (AND MEG)

Positively can do…
All the things that
make us…

It'll be a good chance to get away from the evil monkey that lives in my closet.

Chris brings up his nemesis.

Season 2, Episode 21: "Fore, Father"
"The Best Chris Griffin Quotes From *Family Guy*", ranker.com

Sometimes, it's really hard being me. So, I guess I just make Meganade.

Meg explains her approach to life.

Season 9, Episode 12: "The Hand That Rocks the Wheelchair"
"*Family Guy*: Meg Griffin's Best Quotes, Ranked", movieweb.com

FACTILY GUY

Lacey Chabert played Meg during the first season before being replaced by Mila Kunis.

When Brian and Stewie travel in time to the first episode in "Back to the Pilot", Stewie notes, "Oh my God, what's with Meg's voice? She sounds like someone who's about to give up a huge opportunity."

Chris: See, my dad's smarter than yours.
Meg: We have the same dad, lardo.
Chris: Yeah, but mine's smarter.

Meg points out Chris' flawed logic.

Season 4, Episode 6: "Petarded"
"The Best Chris Griffin Quotes From *Family Guy*", ranker.com

I just want peace on Earth. That's better than Meg, right? So I should get more than her.

Chris tells Lois what he wants for Christmas.

Season 3, Episode 16: "A Very Special Family Guy Freakin' Christmas"
"Family Guy: Chris' 5 Funniest Quotes (& Meg's 5 Funniest)", screenrant.com

Photographer: Listen, you probably get asked this all the time, but have you ever modelled?
Meg: I've never even been in a picture before.

Meg is asked about her previous modelling experience.

Season 13, Episode 9: "This Little Piggy"
"*Family Guy*: Chris' 5 Funniest Quotes (& Meg's 5 Funniest)", screenrant.com

Peter: Why Cheesie Charlie's?

Chris: It's cool, Dad. They have this game where you put in a dollar and you win four quarters. I win every time.

Chris reflects on his favourite arcade game.

Season 1, Episode 3: "Chitty Chitty Death Bang"
"The Best Chris Griffin Quotes From *Family Guy*", ranker.com

66

There he is, the reason my bedpost is so shiny.

99

Meg spots her crush, Kent Lastname.

Season 11, Episode 7: "Friends Without Benefits"
"*Family Guy*: Chris' 5 Funniest Quotes (& Meg's 5 Funniest)", screenrant.com

Can't we eat? I'm so hungry, I could ride a horse… I don't get it… well I could ride it to the store, I guess.

Chris muddles his way through an idiom.

Season 3, Episode 3: "Mr. Griffin Goes to Washington"
"Family Guy: Chris' 5 Funniest Quotes (& Meg's 5 Funniest)", screenrant.com

Meg: You could kill all the girls who are prettier than me.
Death: Well, that would just leave England.

Meg has a request for the Grim Reaper.

Season 2, Episode 6: "Death Is a Bitch"
"Family Guy: Meg Griffin's Best Quotes, Ranked", movieweb.com

FACTILY GUY

According to the
Season 12 episode
"A Fistful of Meg", Meg's
first name isn't "Meg",
but "Megatron", after
Peter doctored her
birth certificate.

Meg: Dad, stop. Even I can see that your sister's a huge bully. And trust me, I know more about getting bullied than anyone.
Peter: You do? How?

Meg admits to Peter that she has suffered bullying.

Season 14, Episode 6: "Peter's Sister"
imdb.com

Chris: Dad, you should invent the frisbee.

Brian: They already invented that.

Chris: Then how come I never heard of it!

Chris gives his father toy-making advice.

Season 2, Episode 7: "The King Is Dead"
"Family Guy: 10 Of Chris Griffin's Most Hilarious Quotes", screenrant.com

Dear my boyfriend, thank you for making out with me recently, on purpose. That was cool. Those flowers that you totally sent me were really pretty. Just like you said I am. Love, Meg.

Meg recites an e-mail to her totally-not-made-up boyfriend.

Season 5, Episode 13: "Bill & Peter's Bogus Journey"
"*Family Guy*: Chris' 5 Funniest Quotes (& Meg's 5 Funniest)", screenrant.com

Chris: Hey, Dad, are you busy? I was thinking we could spend some time together.
Peter: OK, are you a television set or the internet?
Chris: No.
Peter: Oh, then no.

Chris request for quality time is rejected by Peter.

Season 12, Episode 14: "Fresh Heir"
"Peter Griffin Quotes", quotecatalog.com

Sorry, Meg. Daddy loves you,
but Daddy also loves *Star Trek*,
and in all fairness, *Star Trek*
was here first.

Meg blocks Peter's view of the TV.

Season 1, Episode 2: "I Never Met the Dead Man"
"17 Hilarious Moments From *Family Guy* That Prove It's Time For
A Rewatch", ranker.com

Hey, Dad, look! I covered my back with honey, and now the ants are taking me home.

Chris struggles to get the hang of camping.

Season 2, Episode 21: "Fore, Father"
"The Best Chris Griffin Quotes From *Family Guy*", ranker.com

Meg: I just wanna kill myself! I'm going upstairs right now and eat a whole bowl of peanuts… I'm allergic to peanuts. You don't know anything about me!
Peter: Who was that guy?

"

Meg finds out that her parents don't know about her allergies.

Season 3, Episode 8: "The Kiss Seen Around the World"
familyguy.fandom.com

His brain ain't right, but it's fun.

Chris and his "Hamster Dance Tourette's Syndrome" is observed (and judged) by Stewie.

Season 13, Episode 11: "Encyclopedia Griffin"
"Stewie Griffin Quotes", quotecatalog.com

Meg: Oh my god! I'm missing the news!

Peter: We all miss the news, Meg. But Huey Lewis needs time to create and we have to learn to be patient.

Meg's desire to watch *Quahog 5 News* is misinterpreted by Peter.

Season 3, Episode 8: "The Kiss Seen Around the World"
familyguy.fandom.com

Anna: I'm really sorry about your dad's parrot.
Chris: Well, that's OK. He'll get over it pretty quickly and then move to another wacky thing.

Chris is realistic about his father's changing obsessions.

Season 6, Episode 12: "Long John Peter"
"60 Best *Family Guy* Quotes We Love", toynk.com

FACTILY GUY

In his audition for Chris, Seth Green based his vocal performance on the character of Buffalo Bill from *The Silence of the Lambs*.

Chris: I don't have to listen to you! You're a dog! You don't have a soul!
Brian: Ouch!

Chris hurts Brian's feelings.

Season 4, Episode 1: "North by North Quahog"
"The Best Chris Griffin Quotes From *Family Guy*", ranker.com

You know, Meg, if you kill yourself now, you'll probably get a full page in the yearbook. 🙶🙶

Meg receives advice from Stewie.

Season 4, Episode 8: "8 Simple Rules for Buying My Teenage Daughter"
familyguy.fandom.com

Brian: If I remember correctly, this is the physics department.
Chris: That explains all the gravity.

Chris goes on a tour of Brian's old university.

Season 2, Episode 19: "The Story on Page One"
"The Best Chris Griffin Quotes From *Family Guy*", ranker.com

Peter: I'm sick of Lois' anger management techniques. They're not working.

Brian: What about the 'writing angry letters and not sending them' exercise?

Peter: Aww, Jeez, I wasn't supposed to send those?

Meg: Hey look, I got a letter from Dad! 'Dear Meg, for the first four years of your life, I thought you were a house cat.'

Meg receives a letter from her father.

Season 3, Episode 7: "Lethal Weapons"
tvfanatic.com

There is a room where
you can go in and just get free
people!

Chris visits a maternity ward.

Season 15, Episode 15: "Cop and a Half-Wit"
"Family Guy: 10 Of Chris Griffin's Most Hilarious Quotes", screenrant.com

Meg: So, anyone wanna ask me about my week? Kind of a big week for the Megster... Big envelope in the mail... Yep, early admittance... Day 1, August 26th. Clean slate.
Peter: Closing credits.

Meg shows up late to the episode.

Season 18, Episode 8: "Short Cuts"
"*Family Guy*: Meg Griffin's Best Quotes, Ranked", movieweb.com

CHAPTER
FIVE

STEWIE GRIFFIN

Laugh and cry

66

What the deuce?

99

Stewie's catchphrase throughout *Family Guy*.

"Family Guy: 10 Best Stewie Griffin Quotes", screenrant.com

Peter: Run along, Stewie, Daddy had a rough night.

Stewie: Why you tottering fen-sucked dewberry, I'm going to find something to strike you with, excuse me.

Stewie takes out his frustration on Peter.

Season 3, Episode 7: "Lethal Weapons"
"*Family Guy*: Stewie Griffin's 15 Best Quotes, Ranked", movieweb.com

FACTILY GUY

Seth MacFarlane's
voice for Stewie
is inspired
by Rex Harrison in
My Fair Lady.

Mother, I come bearing a gift. I'll give you a hint: it's in my diaper, and it's not a toaster.

Stewie greets Lois.

Season 2, Episode 8: "I Am Peter, Hear Me Roar"
"60 Best *Family Guy* Quotes We Love", toynk.com

May every person that laughs at your sophomoric effort be a reminder of your eternal mediocrity, and pierce your heart like a knife!

Stewie gives his review of Brian's play.

Season 11, Episode 10: "Brian's Play"
"14 of Stewie's Best Insults on *Family Guy*", cracked.com

There's always been a lot of tension between Lois and me. And it's not so much that I want to kill her, it's just… I want her… not to be alive any more.

Stewie sums up his feelings about Lois.

Season 2, Episode 12: "Fifteen Minutes of Shame"
"Stewie Griffin's Best Insults", ign.com

Meg: Everybody! Guess what I am?

Stewie: The end result of a drunken back-seat grope-fest and a broken prophylactic?

Stewie calls it as he sees it.

Season 3, Episode 5: "And the Wiener Is..."
"*Family Guy*: Meg Griffin's Best Quotes, Ranked", movieweb.com

"

Oh, yes, Meg. Yes, yes, yes, everything was going swimmingly for you until this. Yes, yes, this is the thing that will ruin your reputation, not your years of grotesque appearance or awkward social graces, or that Felix Unger-ish way you clear your sinuses. No, no, it's this. Do you hear yourself talk? I might kill you tonight.

"

Stewie points out some truths after Meg expresses dismay at Peter's embarrassing diagnosis.

Season 4, Episode 6: "Petarded"
"Stewie Griffin's Best Insults", ign.com

Listen, you, I'll use these facilities when I'm damn well ready! Until then, you shall continue to sanitize my crevasse and be damn grateful for the opportunity! Starting right... well, not now... but soon!

Stewie resists the call of toilet training.

Season 2, Episode 4: "Brian in Love"
"Stewie Griffin's Best Insults", ign.com

Stewie: Blast you, woman! Awake
from your damnable reverie!

Lois: Honey, I'm doing the dishes.

Stewie: Oh, well, a thousand pardons
for disrupting your flatware
sanitation ritual. But you see, I'm in
searing pain!

Lois: Oh, you're just teething, Stewie.
It's a normal part of a baby's life.

Stewie: Very well then. I order you
to kill me at once!

Stewie is upset that he's started teething.

Season 1, Episode 4: "Mind Over Murder"
"Stewie Griffin Quotes", quotecatalog.com

Brian: Say something.
Stewie: What?
Brian: Just say something, please!
Stewie: Oh for god's sake. Umm. Yeah and God said to Abraham, 'You will kill your son Isaac.' And Abraham said, 'I can't hear you, you'll have to speak into the microphone.' And God said, 'Oh I'm sorry, is this better? Check check check. Jerry, pull the high end out, I'm still getting some hiss back here.'

Brian pushes Stewie to give a moving eulogy for his mother's funeral.

Season 2, Episode 13: "Road to Rhode Island"
imdb.com

You know what?
I'm gonna buy a cake when
you're dead.

Stewie reacts to criticism from Brian.

Season 8, Episode 14: "Peter-assment"
"*Family Guy*: 10 Best Stewie Griffin Quotes", screenrant.com

I'm free! Free from the spell of those diabolical Teletubbies! Thank you. When the world is mine, your death shall be quick and painless.

Stewie is grateful that Peter has changed the channel.

Season 1, Episode 5: "A Hero Sits Next Door"
"*Family Guy*: Stewie Griffin's 15 Best Quotes, Ranked", movieweb.com

FACTILY GUY

Mort and Muriel's son,
Neil Goldman, is
named after one of the
show's writers (the one
whose name is Neil
Goldman).

Damn you, vile woman! You've impeded my work since the day I escaped from your wretched womb.

Stewie insults Lois.

Season 1, Episode 1: "Death Has a Shadow"
"Stewie's Best Insults on *Family Guy*", cracked.com

> **"**
> You know, Mother, as first lady of the American stage Helen Hayes once said, 'I'm going to kill you!'
> **"**

Stewie is upset at Lois after auditioning for her play.

Season 2, Episode 7: "The King Is Dead"
"*Family Guy*: Stewie Griffin's 15 Best Quotes, Ranked", movieweb.com

Olivia: Stewie, you're being mean.

Stewie: No, if I was being mean, when you opened the door, I would've said, 'Oh, hey, Ray Liotta, is Olivia home? You see, I thought you were Ray Liotta because your skin has the texture of a decorative autumn squash.'

Stewie is mean to his crush.

Season 5, Episode 7: "Chick Cancer"
"Stewie Griffin's Best Insults", ign.com

If I see one onion on there,
you can forget about the $1.80
tip you need to live.

Stewie gives his order to a waiter.

Season 11, Episode 9: "Space Cadet"
"14 of Stewie's Best Insults on *Family Guy*", cracked.com

The only reason we die
is because we accept it as
an inevitability.

Stewie is under the influence after he visits
Amsterdam with Brian.

Season 3, Episode 20: "Road to Europe"
"60 Best *Family Guy* Quotes We Love", toynk.com

How does it feel to be
the least cultured person
at a bus station?

Stewie insults Brian.

Season 11, Episode 21: "Roads to Vegas"
"14 of Stewie's Best Insults on *Family Guy*", cracked.com

FACTILY GUY

Stewie is his own ancestor. In the Season 9 episode "The Big Bang Theory", his half-brother Bertram kills Leonardo da Vinci to prevent Stewie from being born, so Stewie injects Leonardo's girlfriend with his own DNA.

Stewie: Lois? Lois? Lois? Lois? Lois? Mom? Mom? Mom? Mommy? Mommy? Mommy? Momma? Momma? Momma? Ma? Ma? Ma? Ma? Mom? Mom? Mom? Mom? Mommy? Mommy? Momma? Momma? Momma?
Lois: WHAT?
Stewie: Hi.

Stewie tries to get Lois' attention.

Season 5, Episode 1: "Stewie Loves Lois"
"Stewie Griffin Quotes", quotecatalog.com

I... I... I love you. I mean, you know, not in like a, 'Hey, let's, you know, let's have an underpants party,' or whatever grown-ups do when they're in love, but I mean, I mean, I love you as one loves another person whom one simply cannot do without.

Stewie confesses his true feelings to Brian.

Season 8, Episode 17: "Brian & Stewie"
"Brian & Stewie Quotes", familyguy.fandom.com

"

Lois: Stewie, why don't you play in the other room?
Stewie: Why don't you burn in hell?

"

Stewie confesses his true feelings to Lois.

Season 1, Episode 1: "Death Has a Shadow"
"Lois Griffin Quotes", allgreatquotes.com

CHAPTER
SIX

QUAGMIRE
AND OTHER
QUAHOGIANS

He's a Family Guy!

"

Giggity giggity goo!

"

Quagmire's catchphrase throughout *Family Guy*.

"*Family Guy*: Quagmire's 5 Funniest Quotes (& Joe's 5 Funniest)",
screenrant.com

What the hell? You're not the same giraffe from last night! Get out of here!

Quagmire reacts to Peter's new giraffe poking its head into his room.

Season 5, Episode 0: "Barely Legal"
"*Family Guy*: Quagmire's 5 Funniest Quotes (& Joe's 5 Funniest)",
screenrant.com

Pretend I'm your child, Lois… Not Meg! Not Meg!

Joe needs rescuing by Lois after a helicopter crash.

Season 4, Episode 9: "Breaking Out Is Hard to Do"
"*Family Guy*: Quagmire's 5 Funniest Quotes (& Joe's 5 Funniest)",
screenrant.com

Peter: Say, what happened to the car wash thief?

Joe: Ironically, I severed his spine when I landed on him.

Peter: Looks like you got more competition at next year's special people's games, huh?

Joe: Nope, he's dead.

Joe takes down another criminal.

Season 3, Episode 15: "Ready, Willing, and Disabled"
"The Best Joe Swanson Quotes From *Family Guy*", ranker.com

What the hell? No, no, no, no, no! I got to stop taking my baths during Peter's shenanigans.

Cleveland's bathtub plummets after the front of his house is destroyed.

Season 5, Episode 8: "Barely Legal"
"The Most Hilarious Cleveland Brown Quotes", ranker.com

> **"**
> Your kid's got a walk-in closet?! Two of mine gotta sleep in the car!
> **"**

Cleveland is shocked by Peter's relative affluence.

Season 13, Episode 11: "Encyclopedia Griffin"
"The Most Hilarious Cleveland Brown Quotes", ranker.com

I love this job more than I love taffy, and I'm a man who enjoys his taffy.

Mayor Adam West expresses his passion for chewy candy.

Season 2, Episode 18: "E. Peterbus Unum"
imdb.com

Doctor: Mayor West, you have lymphoma.
Mayor West: Oh, my.
Doctor: Probably from rolling around in
that toxic waste.
Mayor West: I see.
Doctor: What in God's name were you trying
to prove?
Mayor West: I was trying to gain super
powers.
Doctor: Well, that's just silly.
Mayor West: Silly? Yes. Idiotic? Yes.

Mayor Adam West has an unexpected side effect
from trying to become a superhero.

Season 3, Episode 21: "Family Guy Viewer Mail #1"
familyguy.fandom.com

Do you know who I am?
I'm Tom Tucker, damn it! I make more in an hour than you make in two hours!

Tom Tucker shows off when he doesn't get a reserved seat.

Season 11, Episode 10: "Brian's Play"
tvfanatic.com

Good evening, I'm Tom Tucker.
Coming up, important traffic
news that can't help you because
you're some place where
a TV is.

Tom Tucker introduces the news.

Season 6, Episode 9: "Back to the Woods"
imdb.com

Whoa, whoa, whoa. All right, look: everyone but Chris keep your pants on and let's figure a way out of this.

Herbert the Pervert tries to calm everyone down.

Season 9, Episode 1: "And Then There Were Fewer"
"Top 10 Best *Family Guy* Quotes", thetoptens.com

You're starting to piss me off, you little piggly son of a bitch. Call me.

Herbert has mixed feelings about Chris.

Season 3, Episode 12: "To Love and Die in Dixie"
"Top 10 Best 'Herbert the Pervert' Quotes", thetoptens.com

Diane Simmons: …and reports indicate she has also consumed a record amount of seamen.
Tom Tucker: Well that sounds like one powerful hurricane, Diane.

Diane Simmons and **Tom Tucker** report on a natural disaster.

Season 3, Episode 8: "The Kiss Seen Around the World"
tvfanatic.com

Diane Simmons: Our top story tonight, I will be playing the role of Anna in the Quahog Players' production of *The King and I*. Tom?

Tom Tucker: Thanks, Diane. In other news, I won't be going to the play because I'm sure it will be lousy.

Diane Simmons makes a personal announcement.

Season 2, Episode 7: "The King Is Dead"
imdb.com

Ooh, a quarter! I don't care
what that doctor found
on my nuts, today's going
to be a good day!

Mort Goldman looks on the bright side.

Season 11, Episode 4: "Yug Ylimaf"
familyguy.fandom.com

Aww, zip it, egghead. You with your big words and your… and your small, difficult words.

Mort Goldman is defied by Peter.

Season 3, Episode 21: "Family Guy Viewer Mail #1"
foreverdreaming.com

Jillian: Think about this: have you ever seen the sun and the moon at the same time?
Peter: They're the same person!

Jillian and Peter find that their brains are similar.

Season 5, Episode 5: "Whistle While Your Wife Works"
imdb.com

Stewie: I want some more of Jillian's delicious lemonade!

Jillian: I know, it's good right? I just wish they didn't have to kill so many lemons to make it.

Jillian doesn't quite understand how lemonade works.

Season 5, Episode 5: "Whistle While Your Wife Works"
imdb.com

Tom Tucker: And now here's Ollie Williams with the BlaccuWeather forecast. Ollie?
Ollie Williams: It's gon' rain!
Tom Tucker: Thanks, Ollie.

Ollie Williams gives the weather report.

Season 3, Episode 9: "Mr. Saturday Knight"
imdb.com

Tom Tucker: Let's go live to Ollie Williams with the BlaccuWeather report. Ollie?

Ollie Williams: It's raining sideways!

Tom Tucker: Sounds rough, Ollie. Do you have an umbrella?

Ollie Williams: Had one!

Tom Tucker: Where is it?

Ollie Williams: Inside out, two miles away!

Tom Tucker: Is there anything we can do for you?

Ollie Williams: Bring me some soup!

Tom Tucker: What kind?

Ollie Williams: Chunky!

Ollie Williams does a field report during a hurricane.

Season 4, Episode 12: "Perfect Castaway"
familyguy.fandom.com

Bonnie: I don't want to bring a
new baby into the world with him
running around.
Peter: OK, first of all, Bonnie, you've
been pregnant for like, six years,
all right? Either have the baby
or don't.

Bonnie's unusually long pregnancy is pointed out by
Peter.

Season 4, Episode 3: "Blind Ambition"
familyguy.fandom.com

Meg: Thanks for being so understanding. I hope I didn't get you into too much trouble. I mean, you're not going to go to jail or anything, are you?

Bonnie: No, I'll be around. I need these voice-over checks to support my gambling addiction.

Bonnie elbows the fourth wall.

Season 9, Episode 12: "The Hand That Rocks the Wheelchair"
familyguy.fandom.com

Peter: Hiya, Mr Pewterschmidt.

Carter Pewterschmidt: Peter, I see you're still fatter than holy hell.

Peter: You can read me like a book.

Carter Pewterschmidt greets his son-in-law.

Season 4, Episode 10: "Model Misbehavior"
imdb.com

Carter Pewterschmidt: You look familiar.

Gardener: I was your gardener for twelve years.

Carter Pewterschmidt: Oh. You look different without my lawn under you.

Gardener: I don't take the lawn with me when I go.

Carter Pewterschmidt: Well, I was right to trust you with it then.

Carter Pewterschmidt meets an old employee.

Season 4, Episode 24: "Peterotica"
imdb.com

Well, Ms. Quagmire, your brother, Glenn, is lucky to be alive. You know, we're all lucky to be alive on such a beautiful day. In fact, nurse, all surgeries are outside today.

Dr. Hartman delivers some good news.

Season 10, Episode 3: "Screams of Silence: The Story of Brenda Q"
familyguyfanon.fandom.com

Lois: Dr. Hartman, do you think the brain tumour might explain why Brian's been acting so odd lately?

Dr. Hartman: Hmm, well I haven't heard of brains being linked to behaviour, but I suppose anything is possible.

Dr. Hartman gives his expert opinion.

Season 13, Episode 8: "Our Idiot Brian"
tvfanatic.com

169

Tricia Takanawa: Here comes Mayor Adam West himself. Mr. West, do you have any words for our viewers?

Mayor West: Yes. Box, toaster, aluminium, maple syrup – no, I take that one back. I'm gonna hold on to that one.

Tricia Takanawa: Thank you, Mayor West.

Tricia Takanawa interviews **Mayor West** on the red carpet.

Season 4, Episode 28: "Stewie B. Goode"
imdb.com

Tom, I'm standing in the bedroom of Judy and Glenn Isaacs. Ten years married and still in love. What's their secret? Judy has an inoperable brain tumour the size of my fist. And that just happens to be Glenn's fetish.

Tricia Takanawa delivers a special report on sex.

Season 2, Episode 4: "Brian in Love"
imdb.com

Quagmire: So, were you like, in an accident, or what?
Seamus: No. Me father was a tree.

Quagmire gets to the bottom of **Seamus Levine**'s whole thing.

Season 3, Episode 10: "A Fish Out of Water"
familyguyfanon.fandom.com

Quagmire: Seamus, my man!

Seamus: Oh, hello. Allow me to introduce you to my son, Woody.

Quagmire: Hey, Woody.

Woody: Hey.

Seamus: He's gonna be a new character on the show.

Quagmire: You're barely a character on the show.

Seamus: More than Woody!

Seamus introduces Quagmire to his son.

Season 18, Episode 9: "Christmas Is Coming"
foreverdreaming.com

Barbara Pewterschmidt: Darling, it's so wonderful to be here.

Carter Pewterschmidt: Yeah, right. The drive here is like a counter-clockwise trip around the Monopoly board.

Carter and **Barbara Pewterschmidt** visit their daughter.

Season 16, Episode 3: "Nanny Goats"
imdb.com

Lois: Mom, would you have sex with Peter?

Barbara Pewterschmidt: Of course, dear.

Lois: Really?

Barbara Pewterschmidt: Carter's been most insufferable lately, and this would just stick in his craw.

Peter: I like your freaky spirit, but it's your craw I'm after.

Lois: I didn't think you'd be so receptive.

Barbara Pewterschmidt: Are you kidding, Lois? I'm physically starved. Your father's utterly lost interest. He won't even look me in the back of the head any more.

Barbara Pewterschmidt agrees to sleep with her son-in-law.

Season 5, Episode 13: "Bill & Peter's Bogus Journey"
imdb.com

You know, Dr. Hartman once told me I had gonorrhoea, so I hit him in the head with a bat. I give gonorrhoea, I don't get gonorrhoea, OK?

Quagmire tells Peter that he doesn't have to listen to Dr. Hartman.

Season 12, Episode 9: "Peter Problems"
imdb.com

Bonnie: Somebody save him, he can't swim!

Peter: Oh, he's not even kicking. Kick, Joe, kick!

Lois: Peter, he's a paraplegic!

Peter: That doesn't mean he can't hear. Kick, Joe, kick!

Peter gives advice after Joe falls off a yacht.

Season 4, Episode 5: "The Cleveland–Loretta Quagmire"
"Lois Griffin Quotes", allgreatquotes.com

Quagmire: Oh, God, I gotta get out of this marriage. Cleveland, how did you get out of yours? **Cleveland:** You slept with my wife.

Quagmire forgets how Cleveland's marriage ended.

Season 4, Episode 21: "I Take Thee Quagmire"
"The Most Hilarious Cleveland Brown Quotes", ranker.com

I should warn you: I have a tiny bulletproof shield the exact size of a bullet, somewhere on my body. And if you hit it, I'll be unharmed and your plan will be foiled. You'll be the laughing stock of me.

Mayor West is well protected.

Season 4, Episode 25: "You May Now Kiss the... Uh... Guy Who Receives"
familyguy.fandom.com

Stewie: Oh my God, Super Mario.
   What are you doing here?
Mario: I jump on the turtles, Stewie.
   It is not an exciting life, but it is
   my life.

Stewie meets Mario.

Season 11, Episode 6: "Lois Comes Out of Her Shell"
"Stewie Griffin Quotes", quotecatalog.com

Dennis Miller: I don't want to go on a rant here, but America's foreign policy makes about as much sense as Beowulf having sex with Robert Fulton at the first battle of Antietam. I mean, when a neo-conservative defenestrates, it's like Raskolnikov filibuster deoxymonohydroxinate.
Peter: What the hell does 'rant' mean?

Peter watches Dennis Miller on television.

Season 3, Episode 14: "Peter: Husband, Father... Brother?"
familyguy.fandom.com

Tom Tucker: All right, question number one: would you consider growing a moustache?

Interviewee: I guess so?

Tom Tucker: Question number two. Look at my moustache. Do you think it tickles women when I kiss them?

Interviewee: I… I don't know.

Tom Tucker: Wrong. The answer is, oh, only slightly. Only slightly.

Tom Tucker interviews potential *Quahog 5 News* interns.

Season 3, Episode 8: "The Kiss Seen Around the World"
familyguy.fandom.com

Peter: Until you bring the Gumbels back, I am going on a hunger strike. How about that, Callaghan? Can you live with that on your conscience? ...You gonna eat that stapler?

Steven C. Callahan: You can't eat a stapler.

Peter: Wanna split it?

Peter's hunger-strike threat to Steven C. Callahan, the head of NBC, doesn't get off to a great start.

Season 2, Episode 9: "If I'm Dyin', I'm Lyin'"
foreverdreaming.com

Tom Tucker: Well, folks, those are our winning numbers. Good luck to all—

Nikki: Twenty-four!

Tom Tucker: No, that's it. We're done. Anyone watching, do not count twenty-four.

Nikki: Pancakes!

Tom Tucker: OK, I don't know what she's doing now. Somebody turn the machine off. Nikki, Nikki, that's good. That's good. Go wait in my car, all right, you did good.

Tom Tucker's new girlfriend Nikki struggles to read out the lottery numbers.

Season 10, Episode 1: "Lottery Fever"
foreverdreaming.com

❝

Olivia Fuller: Shut up, you egotistical jerk!
Stewie: You shut up, you sack-bellied strumpet!
Olivia Fuller: Blimp-headed jackass!
Stewie: Mealy-mouthed crotch pheasant!

❞

Olivia Fuller and her duet partner Stewie get into an argument.

Season 3, Episode 18: "From Method to Madness"
imdb.com

Quagmire: Hey, who wants to play Drink the Beer?

Peter: Right here. [*Peter drinks a beer.*]

Quagmire: You win.

Peter: All right, what do I win?

Quagmire: Another beer!

Peter: Oh, I'm going for the high score.

Quagmire teaches Peter a new game.

Season 1, Episode 1: "Death Has a Shadow"
"How To Drink Like Peter Griffin From *Family Guy*", thrillist.com

Peter: I feel kind of bad, guys.
I promised my wife I wouldn't drink.
Quagmire: Don't feel bad, Peter.
Peter: Gee, I never thought of it
like that!

Quagmire reframes Peter's way of thinking.

Season 1, Episode 1: "Death Has a Shadow"
familyguy.fandom.com

Clare: Now why don't you patch things up with Mr. Griffin by showing him your Legos?

Peter: You got Legos? Aw, sweet! Lois only buys me Mega Bloks.

Lois: They're the same thing, Peter.

Peter: You know what, Lois? They are not the same thing, and the sooner you get that through your thick skull, the sooner we can get this marriage back on track.

Peter is made to apologize to a local boy for beating him up.

Season 5, Episode 11: "The Tan Aquatic with Steve Zissou"
foreverdreaming.com

"

Grab that letter opener over there. I'm going to show you why you should never mail cash.

"

After Lois gets a job at the post office, **Cleveland** shows her the ropes.

Season 14, Episode 17: "Take a Letter"
"The Most Hilarious Cleveland Brown Quotes", ranker.com

"

Hello, 911? It's Quagmire. Yeah. Yeah, yeah, it's in a window this time.

"

Quagmire calls the emergency services.

Season 3, Episode 7: "Lethal Weapons"
"Top 10 Best *Family Guy* Quotes", thetoptens.com

So can the family understand the baby, or what's the deal with that?

Two hundred years into the future, a student asks this question after learning about the short-lived nation of Peteroia.

Season 2, Episode 18: "E. Peterbus Unum"
familyguy.fandom.com

"

Freaking sweet!

"

Peter's catchphrase throughout *Family Guy...*